HALLELUJAH

Emotively, with some freedom

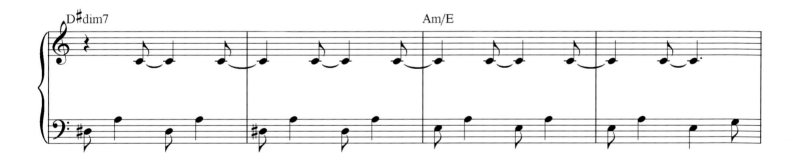

HALLELUJAH

Words and Music by LEONARD COHEN

SONY/ATV MUSIC PUBLISHING LLC

EXCLUSIVELY DISTRIBUTED BY

HAL•LEONARD®
CORPORATION

7777 W. BLUEMOUND RD. P.O. BOX 13819 MILWAUKEE, WI 53213

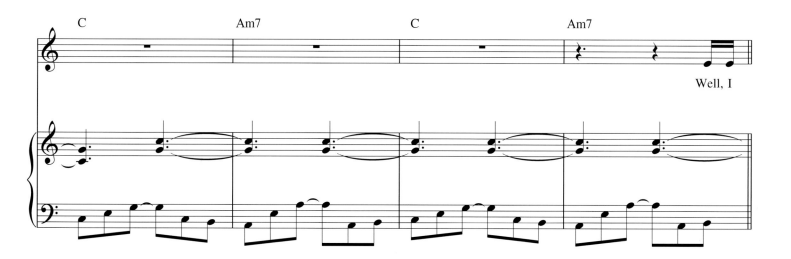

Well, I

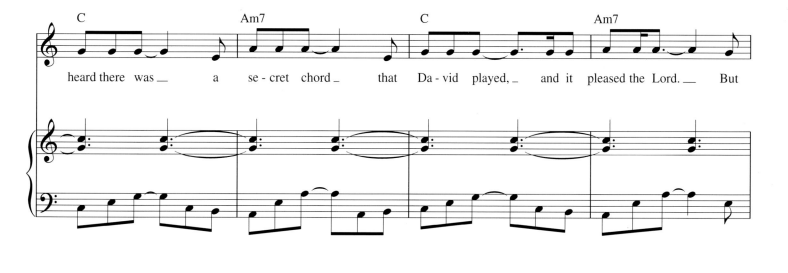

heard there was _ a se - cret chord _ that Da - vid played, _ and it pleased the Lord. _ But

you don't _ real-ly care for mu - sic, do you? _____ Well, it

goes like this: the fourth, the fifth, the mi - nor fall _ and the ma - jor lift, the

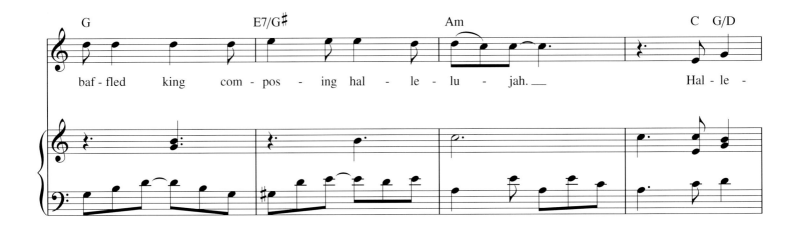

baf - fled king com - pos - ing hal - le - lu - jah. _ Hal - le -

lu - jah, hal - le - lu - jah, hal - le -

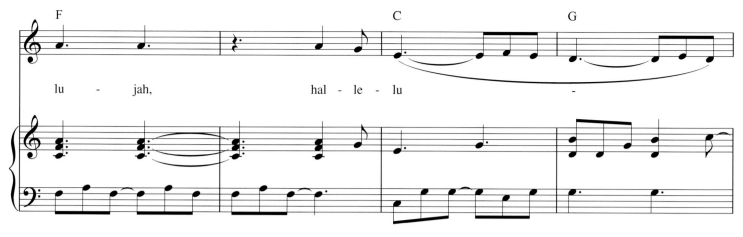

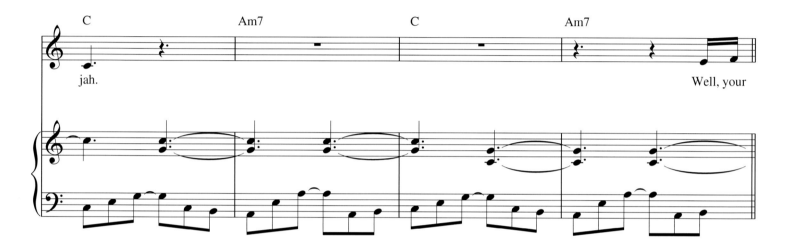

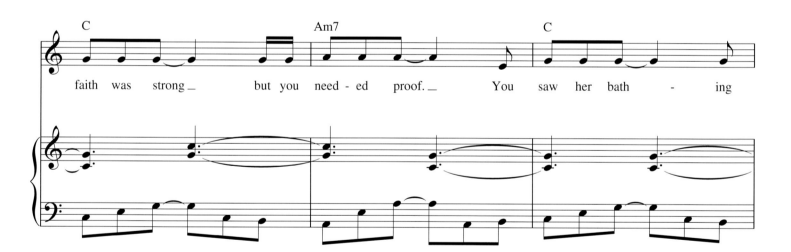

Well, she tied you to her kitch-en chair __ and she

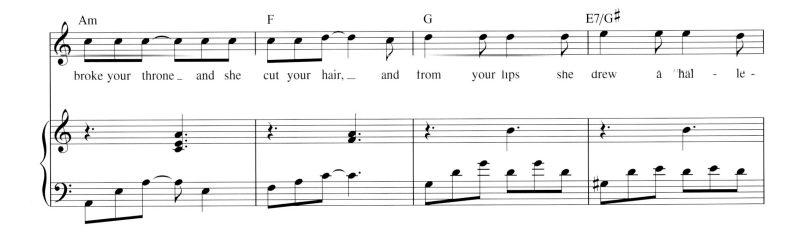

broke your throne __ and she cut your hair, __ and from your lips she drew a "hal - le -

lu - jah." __ Hal - le - lu - jah, hal - le -

lu - jah, hal - le - lu - jah, hal - le -

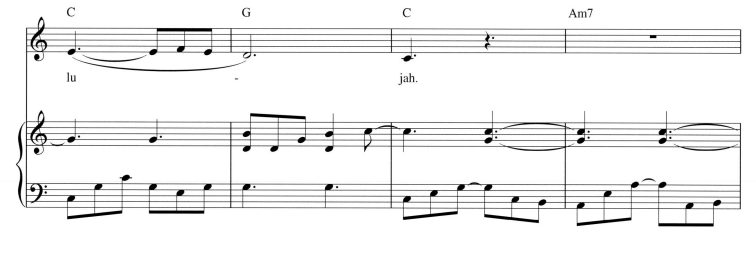

lu - jah.

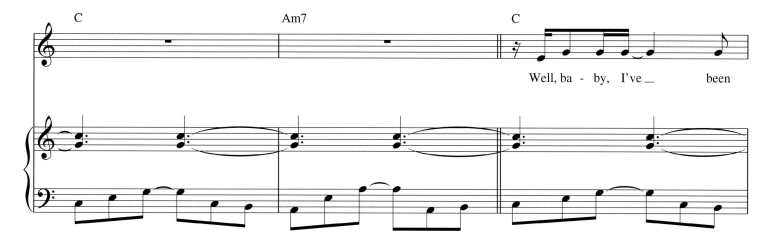

Well, ba - by, I've __ been

here be - fore, I've seen this room and I've walked __ this floor, __ and I,

I used __ to live a - lone __ be - fore I knew you. And I've

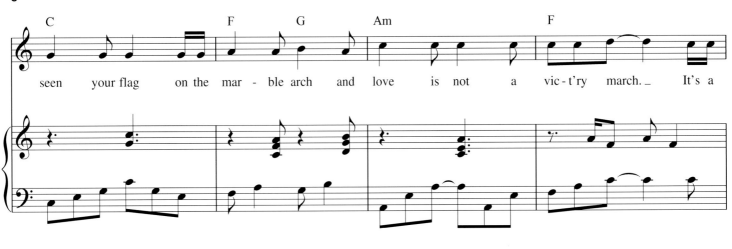

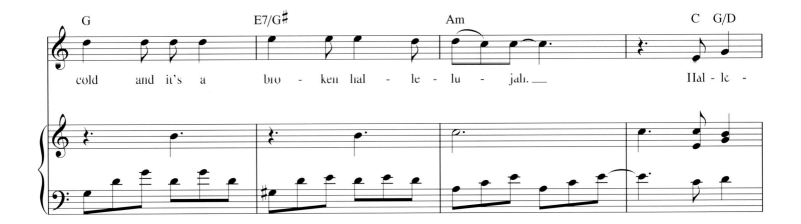

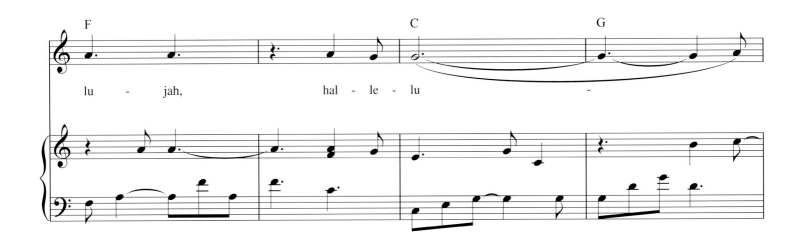

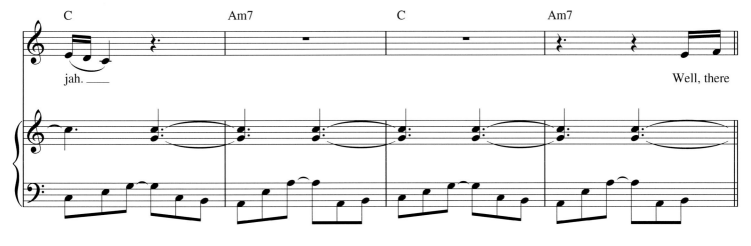

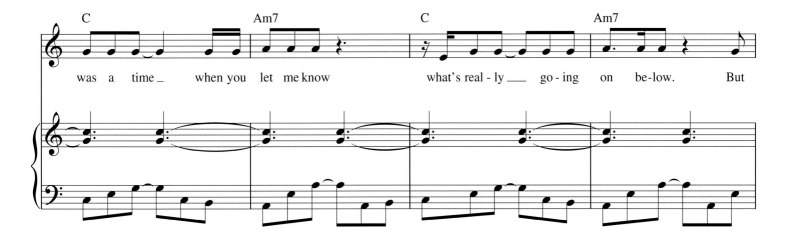

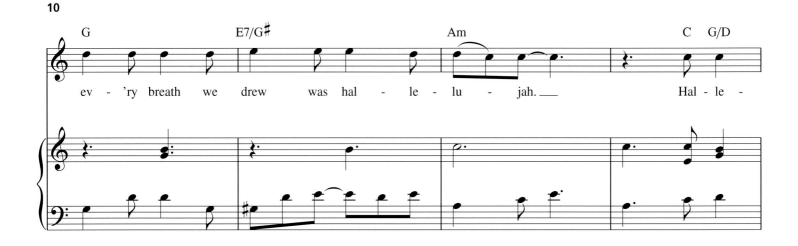

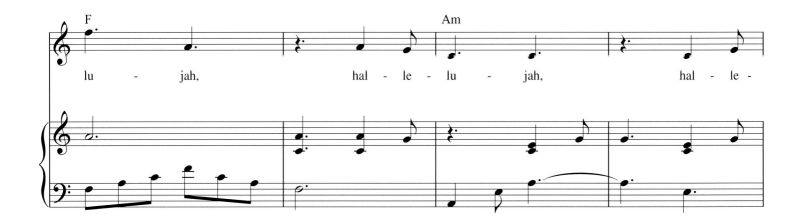

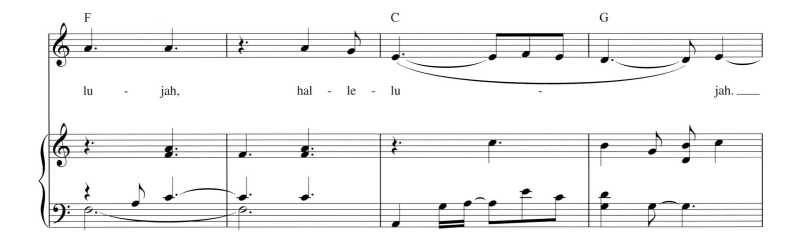

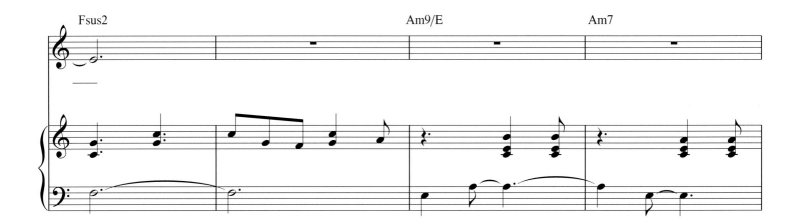

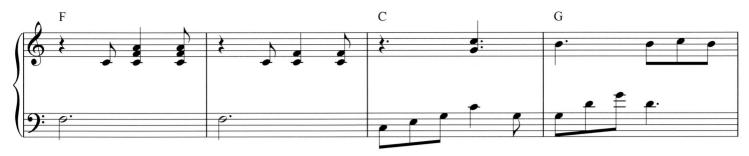

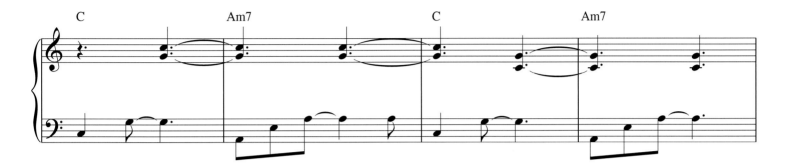

12

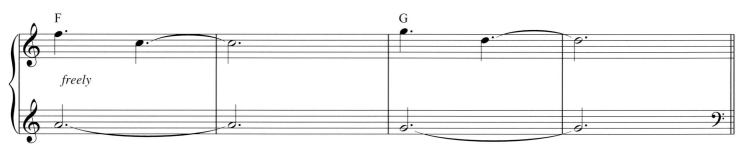

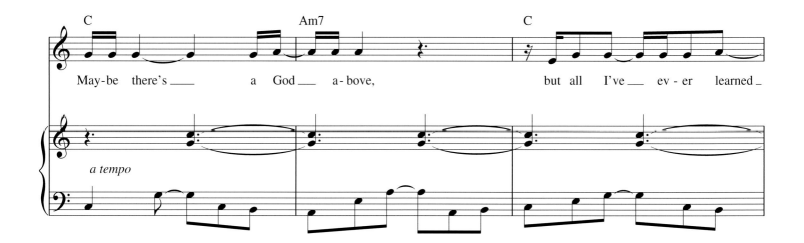

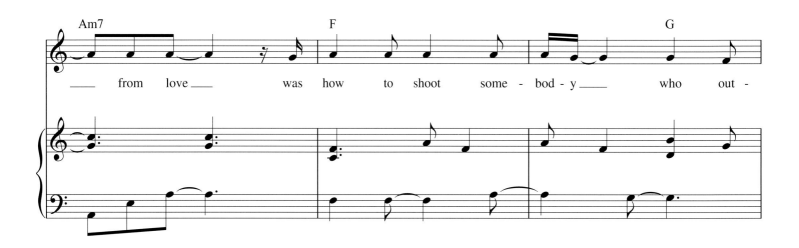

hear at night, it's not some - bod - y who's seen the light._ It's a

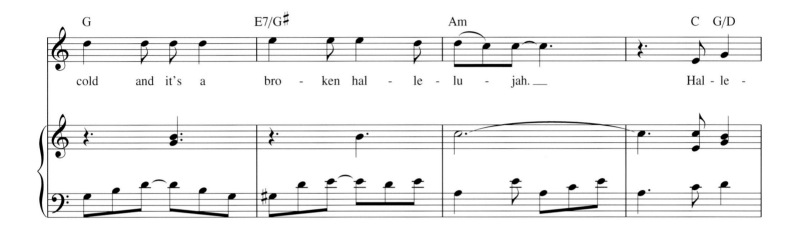

cold and it's a bro - ken hal - le - lu - jah._ Hal - le -

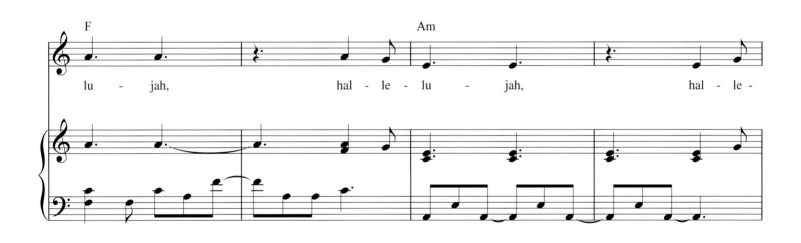

lu - jah, hal - le - lu - jah, hal - le -

lu - jah, hal - le - lu..._ Hal - le -

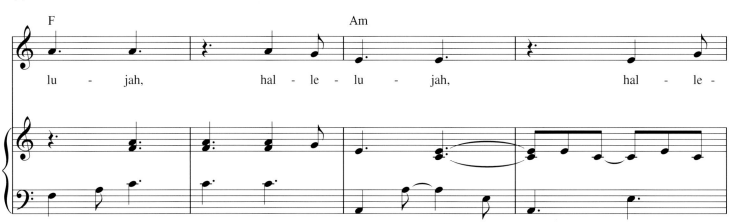

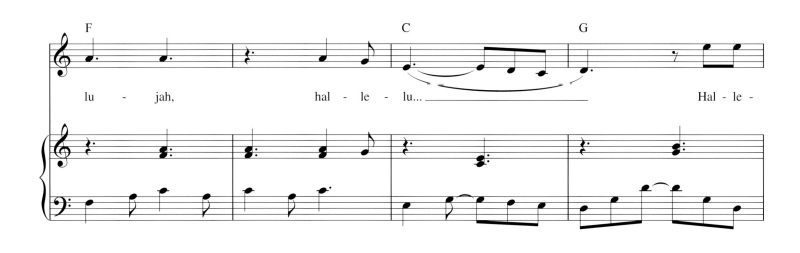

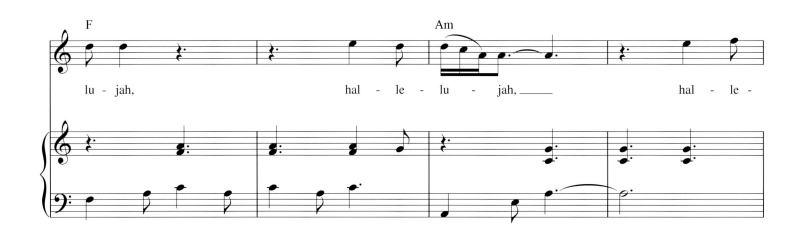

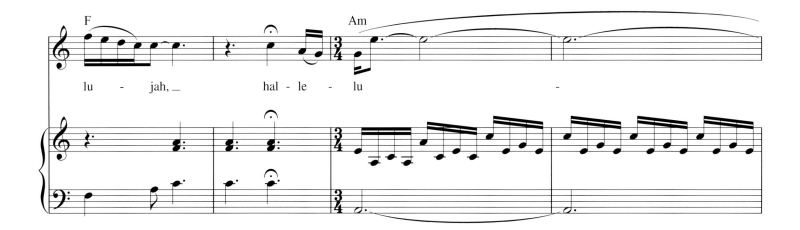

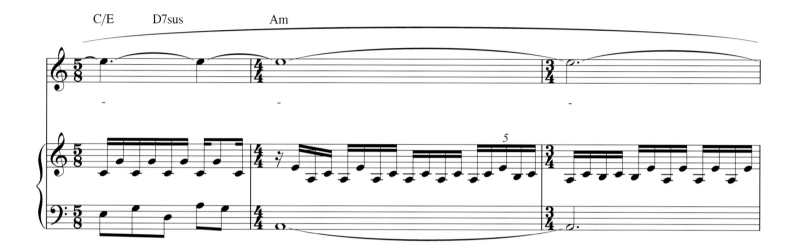

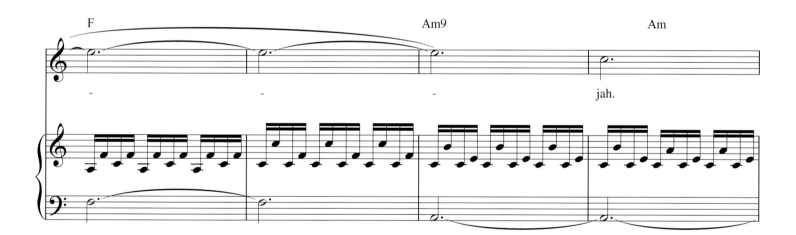

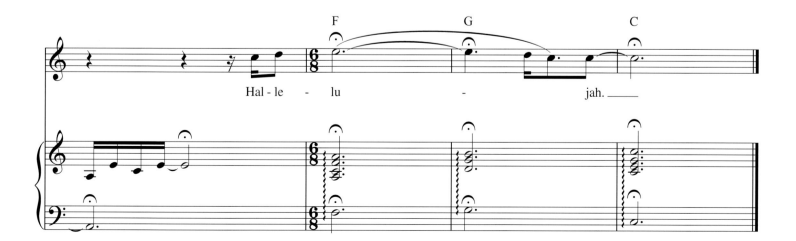